Service
Recovery

Management Master Series

William F. Christopher
Editor in Chief

Set 3: Customer Focus

Karl Albrecht
Delivering Customer Value: It's Everyone's Job

Robert King
Designing Products and Services That Customers Want

Wayne A. Little
Shared Expectations: Sustaining Customer Relationships

Gerald A. Michaelson
Building Bridges to Customers

Eberhard E. Scheuing
Creating Customers for Life

Ron Zemke
Service Recovery: Fixing Broken Customers

Service Recovery

Fixing Broken Customers

Ron Zemke

MANAGEMENT
MASTER
Series

PRODUCTIVITY PRESS
Portland, Oregon

Management Master Series
William F. Christopher, Editor in Chief
Copyright © 1995 by Performance Research Associates, Inc.

Productivity Press
P.O. Box 13390
Portland, OR 97213-0390
United States of America
Telephone: 503-235-0600
Telefax: 503-235-0909
E-mail: staff@ppress.com

Book design by William Stanton
Cover illustration by Paul Zwolak
Graphics and composition by Rohani Design, Edmonds, Washington
Printed and bound by Data Reproductions Corporation in the United
    States of America

Library of Congress Cataloging-in-Publication Data

Zemke, Ron.
      Service recovery : fixing broken customers / Ron Zemke.
          p. cm. — (Management master series)
      Includes bibliographical references and index.
      ISBN 1-56327-150-8 (hardcover)
      ISBN 1-56327-097-8 (paperback)
      1. Customer complaints. 2. Consumer satisfaction. I. Title.
      II. Series.
      HF5415.5.S25   1995
      658.8' 12—dc20   95-12451
                                                                              CIP

00 99 98 97 96 95 10 9 8 7 6 5 4 3 2 1

— CONTENTS —

PUBLISHER'S MESSAGE

The *Management Master Series* was designed to discover and disseminate to you the world's best concepts, principles, and current practices in excellent management. We present this information in a concise and easy-to-use format to provide you with the tools and techniques you need to stay abreast of this rapidly accelerating world of ideas.

World class competitiveness requires managers today to be thoroughly informed about how and what other internationally successful managers are doing. What works? What doesn't? and Why?

Management is often considered a "neglected art." It is not possible to know how to manage before you are made a manager. But once you become a manager you are expected to know how to manage and to do it well, right from the start.

One result of this neglect in management training has been managers who rely on control rather than creativity. Certainly, managers in this century have shown a distinct neglect of workers as creative human beings. The idea that employees are an organization's most valuable asset is still very new. How managers can inspire and direct the creativity and intelligence of everyone involved in the work of an organization has only begun to emerge.

Perhaps if we consider management as a "science" the task of learning how to manage well will be easier. A scientist begins with an hypothesis and then runs experiments to observe whether the hypothesis is correct. Scientists depend on detailed notes about the experiment—the timing, the ingredients, the amounts—and carefully record all results as they test new hypotheses. Certain things come to be known by this method; for instance, that water always consists of one part oxygen and two parts hydrogen.

We as managers must learn from our experience and from the experience of others. The scientific approach provides a model for learning. Science begins with vision and desired outcomes, and achieves its purpose through observation, experiment, and analysis of precisely recorded results. And then what is newly discovered is shared so that each person's research will build on the work of others.

Our organizations, however, rarely provide the time for learning or experimentation. As a manager, you need information from those who have already experimented and learned and recorded their results. You need it in brief, clear, and detailed form so that you can apply it immediately.

It is our purpose to help you confront the difficult task of managing in these turbulent times. As the shape of leadership changes, the *Management Master Series* will continue to bring you the best learning available to support your own increasing artistry in the evolving science of management.

We at Productivity Press are grateful to William F. Christopher and our staff of editors who have searched out those masters with the knowledge, experience, and ability to write concisely and completely on excellence in management practice. We wish also to thank the individual volume authors; Diane Asay, project manager; Julie Zinkus, manuscript editor; Karen Jones, managing editor; Lisa Hoberg and Mary Junewick, editorial support; Bill Stanton, design and production management; Susan Swanson, production coordination; Rohani Design, graphics, page design, and composition.

Norman Bodek
Publisher

INTRODUCTION

The sound of service breakdown is an all too familiar clatter. It happens every time a customer's experience falls short of his or her expectations. The waiter moves in slow motion; the doctor sees a 9:30 appointment at 11:00 am; the flight is late again, the laundry cracks a shirt button; the fax fails, the phone goes dead mid-call. Net-net: The customer is angered by the dissonance between actual and expected performance, and walks away—sometimes forever.

Recovery is a focused effort by a service provider to return the aggrieved customer to a state of satisfaction with the institution after a service or product breakdown. Note carefully the phrase "to a state of satisfaction with the institution." Any customer service person worth his or her salt can mollify an annoyed customer and calm a screaming, ranting, and raving one in short order. When was the last time you heard a service rep say, "Oh, I know, it's just terrible. If it was up to me, I'd give you your money back right now. But they've got this policy and if I break it, well—you know!" That gets the service rep off the spot with the customer, but does little to retain the customer for the organization. Service recovery is about keeping customers coming back after the worst, or at least something very annoying, happens. In simple terms, recovery is the special effort customers expect you to put forward when things have gone wrong for them.

In a perfect world of perfect products and perfect performances, service recovery would be perfectly unnecessary. But ours is not a perfect world; it is a world filled with the mythical Dr. Murphy's gremlins. And when things go wrong, regardless of who caused the problem, the customer expects and demands redress. The true test of an organization's commitment to service quality isn't the stylishness of the pledge it makes in its marketing literature; it is the way the organization responds when things go wrong for the customer.

Effective service recovery, which saves at-risk customers for the organization and becomes a hallmark or competitive distinguisher, is a planned, systematic process. An effective service recovery system is more than an elaborate apology and monetary make-good system designed to mollify upset customers, curry their favor and, if necessary, buy back their business. The core attributes of an effective service recovery system are a problem resolution process, a complaint and problem capture and analysis subsystem, and a way of feeding information on systemic problems back into the system that creates and delivers the service.

This book focuses first on the economic rationale for creating a planned service recovery system, a process of dealing with—and retaining—upset customers. Then it develops guidelines for a service recovery system that becomes a strategic asset and an important part of your total quality effort.

1

THE DOLLARS AND SENSE
OF SERVICE RECOVERY

A growing body of data suggests that companies performing high-quality service recovery for customers can realize substantial economic payoff. According to John Goodman, president of Technical Assistance Research Programs, Inc. (TARP), studies that TARP conducted across numerous industries over the last five years all found that when customers' problems were satisfactorily handled and resolved, their loyalty and repurchase intentions were within a few percentage points of those of customers who had not experienced a product or service failure.[1]

Even more intriguing are four other TARP studies that surveyed industrial customers of a Canadian chemical company, high-value customers of an American bank, customers of two worldwide computer companies, and professional photographers who were customers of a European photographic supply company. These studies found that customers whose complaints are quickly satisfied are more likely to purchase additional products from these companies than are customers who experienced no problems with the organization or with its products (see Figure 1 with regard to the computer companies). In the United States, a TARP study for Polaroid found that customers who telephone to ask about or report problems with camera gear "can be sold additional

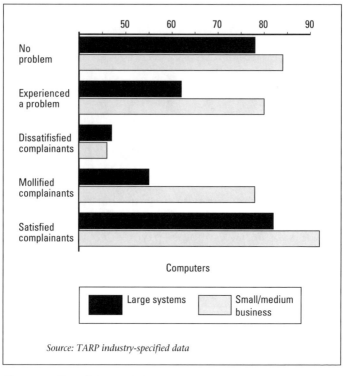

Figure 1. How Many of Your Unhappy Customers Will Buy Other Products or Services Offered by Your Company?

photographic equipment—once the subject of the call has been handled to the customer's satisfaction."[2]

In other words, TARP's research strongly suggests that swift and effective service recovery enhances customers' perception of the quality of the products and services they have already purchased, as well as their perception of the competence of the organization and its personnel. This also enhances the perceived quality and value of other products and services the organization offers.

Leonard L. Berry, who is J.C. Penney Chair of Retailing Studies, professor of marketing, and director of the Center of Retailing Studies at Texas A&M University, and one of the leading service quality researchers in the United States, is equally adamant about the importance of good service recovery: "The acid test of service quality is how you solve customer problems."[3] And though he is cautious—if not skeptical—about Goodman's assertion that good recovery can lead to better than average customer loyalty, he is very sure that the quality of recovery the customer experiences when things go wrong has a strong impact on overall customer satisfaction and customer retention.

Berry explains that a series of studies he and colleagues Valarie A. Zeithaml and A. Parasuraman conducted over the past ten years consistently showed that the best satisfaction scores come from customers who experienced no problems, the second best from those whose problems were resolved satisfactorily, and the worst from customers whose problems remained unsolved. Those differences are statistically and practically significant. The message from all this research is pretty clear: Do it right the first time. If you don't, you'd better be darned sure you do it right the second time. If you fail—if you do not meet the customer's expectations twice—that's about all the room the customer will give you.[4]

Using research models similar to those that TARP and Leonard Berry and his colleagues use, individual businesses are learning about the impact effective service recovery can have on their customers. Research at National Car Rental, for example, found that while there is an 85 percent chance that a satisfied customer will again rent from National, there is a 90 percent probability that a recovered customer will re-rent.[5]

One of the largest hotel corporations in the United States has studied the lost dollar value of unhappy and unrecovered hotel guests. Operation researchers at the company took into account the average number of room nights per year per frequent business-travel customer (the largest and most desirable segment of its customer base), the number of other travelers that an unhappy guest will influence to avoid its properties, the acquisition costs for that original traveler, and the marketing costs involved in replacing that traveler if he or she decides never to use this or any if its properties again. While the exact calculations are proprietary, this corporation believes that the net loss value of one frequent business traveler guest, is equivalent to 81 room nights or $6,480.00.[6] Understanding the impact and the cost in both dollars and sense and the operational terms of losing and replacing a customer for your organization is a critical first step to making service recovery an important strategic tool for your customer service operation.

The impact of poor recovery goes beyond the disappointment and loss of a single customer. The salesperson or customer service rep who dismisses an unhappy or complaining customer with a perfunctory "I can't help you, that's our policy," positions the company to lose dozens, if not hundreds, of current and potential customers. The problem, as the aforementioned hotel company illustrated so clearly, is that the summarily dismissed, complaining customer doesn't simply go away. He or she goes away, stays away, and worse yet, takes every opportunity to tell anyone who will listen about the rotten treatment he or she was made to endure at the hands of your company.

Other research confirms that while 50 percent will complain to the local outlets, as many as 96 percent of unhappy customers won't complain to the head office of the offending business or the manufacturer—but they will tell, on average, nine to ten friends, acquaintances, and colleagues how bad your service is. One study conducted by Performance Research Associates, Inc. found that 18 percent of customers were upset with treatment they received at the hands of a Midwestern phone company. These upset customers reported they each told an average of twenty or more people of their plight. And according to a study conducted by General Electric, there is a significant impact on sales as well. The G.E. study found that "the impact of word of mouth (recommendations from friends and acquaintances) on a customer's repurchase decision is twice as important as corporate advertising.[9]

Frederick Reichheld and W. Earl Sasser have taken the TARP findings one step further.[10] They calculated the value of customer retention over a five-year period for nine industries. Like TARP they considered not only base profit but profit from increased purchases, profit from reduced operating costs (attainable through increased knowledge of a customer's requirements over time), profits from referrals, and profits from price premium purchases. They found that profits from a single customer are not static, but increase over time! A customer who has been with you for 5 years (depending on your industry) can be up to 377 percent more profitable than a customer you have only just wooed to your products or services. Their bottom-line calculation is that by focusing on customer retention tactics, such as service recovery and reducing annual defections by a mere 5 percent, an organization can boost pretax profits 25 percent to 125 percent. The net learning from all this service and dollars research is that focusing on service recovery pays, and pays well.

Finally, TARP has found that while, on average, it costs five times as much to get a new customer as to retain an old one, this five factor actually varies from two to *thirty*, depending on the size of the item (e.g., chewing gum vs. minicomputers) and the complexity of getting a new sale (coupon vs. sales call).

2

WHAT CUSTOMERS EXPECT
WHEN THINGS GO WRONG

Given that service recovery can have such an important and significant impact on the corporate bottom line, it is important to ask: "Just what do unhappy customers want from us?" Most research into what customers require when a company does not meet their initial expectations or breaks promises suggests they want three things:

- What they were promised in the first place
- Some personal attention
- A decent apology

What they don't want is to feel that they caused the problem or are terribly stupid for making a mistake—even though, according to TARP, customers themselves cause an average of 30 percent of the product or service problems they report to companies.[11] Nor do they want their complaints treated as an imposition or nuisance.

Our work suggests strongly that distinctive service recovery involves much more than simply fixing customers' problems when they report them. There is, in fact, an art and a style to doing recovery so well that it is a positive attribute of your organization. Customers have service recovery expectations just as they have expectations of normal product and service performance. In fact, customer research conducted at a number of financial institutions by Linda Cooper of Cooper and Associates, Evanston, IL, suggests that *seven* of the top ten service expectations of bank retail customers relate to the recovery process:

1. Being called back when promised.
2. Receiving an explanation of how a problem happened.*
3. Knowing who to contact with a problem.*
4. Being contacted promptly when a problem is resolved.*
5. Being allowed to talk to someone in authority.
6. Being told how long it will take to resolve a problem.*
7. Being given useful alternatives if a problem can't be solved.*
8. Being treated like a person, not an account number.
9. Being told about ways to prevent a future problem.*
10. Being given progress reports if a problem can't be solved immediately.*

We recently asked, in a slightly different way, what customers expect of the recovery process. Over the past two years, we have conducted focus groups and telephone interviews with over 1,200 customers in a variety

What focus group members remembered and found impressive	% of interviewees who commented on and were impressed by this action
1. CSR* dealt with my upset.	79.0%
2. CSR apologized.	69.1%
3. CSR didn't become defensive, but showed humility and poise.	62.9%
4. CSR followed up after the complaint transaction.	56.8%
5. CSR showed skill at problem solving.	53.0%
6. CSR, when appropriate, was proactive in admitting organization error, didn't try to shift blame.	44.4%
7. CSR acted in a fully responsible and empowered fashion on the customers behalf.	40.7%
8. CSR showed good interpersonal skills, particularly listening.	40.7%
9. CSR showed empathy for the customer's plight and/or upset.	38.3%
10. CSR acted quickly to solve the problem, showed urgency.	35.8%
11. CSR created added value for the customer.	32.1%
12. CSR believed the customer, valued the customer's perception.	24.7%

*CSR= Customer Service Representative

Note: During 1991-1992, Performance Research Associates, Inc., staff members conducted 81 focus group and discussion sessions asking customers what they expected, and what they had experienced as positive, from companies when they experienced a service breakdown. The average group size was 12 discussants, with individual groups ranging from 8 to 20 participants.

Figure 2. What Customers Recall of Effective Service Recovery Incidents

of industries, who recently experienced service break-downs. Our goal was to find out what was most memorable about the service recovery customers encountered. We found that, regardless of the type of service—business to business, consumer, professional, medical—the most memorable aspects of successful service recovery were remarkably similar.

Figure 2 suggests that the most memorable aspects of recovery are almost evenly divided between interpersonal or communications skills (seven items) and technical or problem-focused skills (five items). This leads us to conclude that memorable and organizationally effective service recovery is a fine mix of problem-solving and customer-handling skills.

TARP's research has found that the single most important aspect of a response is a clear, believable explanation of what happened and what will happen.

Based on our and others' research into service recovery, we suggest that service recovery—the act—is at least a six-step process focused on two objectives: Making the customer's problem go away, and doing it in a way that forms a memorable, positive impression on the customer. We discuss this six-step model in the next chapter.

3

SERVICE RECOVERY: THE PROCESS

First and foremost, service recovery is a set of actions that a frontline service person performs to solve a customer problem and keep the customer coming back despite the problem that occurred. Based on our research into positive behaviors and attitudes that customers expect and find memorable about the recovery act and our work with frontline service professionals from dozens of companies, we developed a six-step process for handling disappointed, and even disgruntled, customers. Applied consistently by customer-contact people, it has, in one controlled application, led to an overall 12 percent improvement in customer satisfaction with problem solving.

The Service Recovery Process

1. Acknowledge that the customer is experiencing an inconvenience and apologize for it.

2. Listen, empathize, and ask open questions.

3. Offer a fair fix to the problem.

4. Offer some value-added atonement for the inconvenience or injury.

5. Keep your promises.

6. Follow up.

Step 1. Acknowledge That the Customer Is Experiencing an Inconvenience and Apologize for It

Apologize without becoming defensive or shifting the blame to the customer. This is a key expectation and an important first step toward keeping a customer who feels aggrieved. Although a simple apology costs nothing to deliver, we find it forthcoming in fewer than 48 percent of the cases where a customer reports to a company that a problem exists with a product or service.

Apology is most powerful when delivered *first person singular*. The corporate "We're sorry" form letter lacks the sincerity and authenticity that comes with a personal, verbal acknowledgment delivered on behalf of the organization. A sincere, nonrobotic sounding, "I'm sorry for any inconvenience this late arrival may have caused you" suggests that the pilot, the cabin lead, or whoever is apologizing is taking a personal, professional interest in the situation. And contrary to some fears, apologizing for the customer's inconvenience is not, and cannot be, interpreted as an admission of guilt or acceptance of legal culpability or liability. There is, in fact, some evidence that a simple apology can defuse a situation and prevent escalation.

Apologize without accepting blame: "I'd be unhappy if that happened to me." TARP has found that customer satisfaction increases 10 to 15 percent when the apology sounds genuine.

Step 2: Listen, Empathize, and Ask Open Questions

There is a clear and important difference between *empathy*—acknowledging and understanding the customer's emotional upset—and *sympathy*—sharing that upset, getting angry along with the customer, and engaging in a mutual 'misery fest' with the customer. Customers do not want service professionals to join them in a "those guys in shipping should be shot" tirade. Rather, customers are looking for a good listener who allows them to vent their frustrations, shows understanding of their upset, and who, by listening, offers tacit evidence of believing the customer's report of the incident or error. As we first heard at Digital Equipment Corporation (DEC): "The upset customer doesn't care how much you know, until he knows how much you care."

Step 3. Offer a Fair Fix to the Problem

After the service provider acknowledges and addresses the emotional side of the service breakdown, he or she must correct the customer's problem. It is important that the customer perceives the individual service provider as skilled, empowered, and interested in a timely resolution. And contrary to common belief, customers typically bring a sense of fair play to the table when a situation calls for recompense or compensation. If the service provider offers a rational explanation and demonstrates sensitivity and concern, the customer usually responds in kind.

Asking customers what a fair fix for a problem might be is quite revealing. When we asked telephone subscribers what they expected from the company when service failures occurred, we found they clearly distinguished between a service failure that happened on a weekend and one that happened on a weekday. They told us, in effect, that it was OK for the phone company to be more sluggish in its response on a weekend because, after all, "Sunday is a weekend, and most of them like to be home with their families just like the rest of us."

Providing an explanation of what happened and what will happen *and the rationale* is critical. TARP has found that employees' lack of knowledge of the rationale is the most prevalent failing—and it is easily fixed through training.

Customer expectations of recovery need careful study before an organization embarks on a systematic service recovery effort. Recovery expectations can vary by locale, customer demographics, and who else the customer receives service from in the marketplace. If a large percentage of your customers are also customers of a Nordstrom or a Federal Express, their experiences with those organizations may well have an impact on their expectations and evaluation of you.

Step 4. Offer Some Value-Added Atonement for the Inconvenience/Injury

We often refer to this step as *symbolic atonement.* Symbolic atonement is the free meal, complimentary home delivery, discount coupon, and partial or full refund offer that compensates the customer for the inconvenience. Atonement isn't a *requiremen*t for successful recovery from *every* service or product breakdown. Rather, atonement is critical to satisfaction when the customer feels "injured" by the service delivery breakdown—when the customer feels victimized, greatly inconvenienced, or somehow damaged by the problem.

At the most basic level, atonement is a gesture that clearly says, "We want to make it up to you." Atonement is the "It's on us," "Free drink," "No charge," demonstration of goodwill. The word "symbolic" is carefully chosen. It suggests that little things, when sincerely done, mean a lot to the customer. The customer does *not* expect us to offer to shoot the branch manager or provide a trip to Walt Disney World for keeping him or her waiting in the reception area an extra ten minutes. The customer *does* expect us to make a reasonable small gesture that acknowledges the inconvenience.

There is an easy way to confirm that your own customers have reasonable and modest expectations. Create ten to twenty typical service breakdown scenarios, each ending with the question, "What do we need to do to make things right for this customer and win back his or her loyalty?" Then give the scenarios to ten customers in a focus group and to ten customer service representatives. Our experience is that in the majority of cases, what customers ask for by way of atonement costs less and is easier to deliver than what your service representatives suggest. Customers prove to us over and over again that, by and large, they hold inimically reasonable expectations of recovery in general, and atonement in particular.

Sometimes, however, a custom-tailored or highly aggressive act of atonement might be *necessary* to keep a highly valued customer. And sometimes a determined, proactive effort can both impress the customer and give your organization an extra satisfaction "bump." When management at L.L. Bean, the catalog retailer in Freeport, Maine, learned that a sport shirt it was selling had a tendency to fray at the collar after only a few washings, they took the initiative. Every customer who had purchased the shirt received a letter informing them of the problem and encouraging return of the shirt. The letter further instructed that if returning the shirt was inconvenient, the Bean customer service unit would be pleased to arrange a pick-up for the customers; a gesture that further emphasized the sincerity of Bean's offer.

Step 5. Keep Your Promises

Customers are frequently skeptical of a company's recovery promises. Their tendency is to believe that service representatives' promises aim at getting the customer off the phone or out of the office, rather than actually solving the problem or fixing the customer's upset. Although bad news may prompt the customer to huff and bluster at the customer-contact employee, customers would rather hear bad news than lies or misleading information. For example, customers would rather be informed that their flight may be up to ninety minutes late than be told of a fifteen minute delay six different times. Customers value and share with others the feats of customer service representatives who display a "can do" attitude and ability. On the other hand, they frequently tell horror stories of promises made but broken, often for years after the incident.

Step 6. Follow Up

Customers are also favorably impressed when a sales or customer service person follows up with them after the initial service recovery episode to make sure that the solution is still satisfactory.

This after-the-fact service recovery satisfaction assessment is particularly important in breakdown situations where customers perceive that they may be "at risk" if they voice anger or are upset. For example, research conducted by Philip A. Newbold and Diane Stover of Memorial Hospital in South Bend, Indiana, found that "because of fear of retaliation, some patients kept quiet (about service disappointments) until after discharge, particularly regarding nursing issues."[14] Following up gives the organization a second chance to solve the customer's problem when the first effort falls short of the customer's expectations, and especially if the customer was reluctant to voice the complaint to you a second time.

This step should also initiate an internal follow-up. Service representatives should be able to communicate inside their organizations to ensure that the solutions they put in motion are actually executed (the package was shipped, the account credited), and to allow recurring problems to be tracked and removed from the delivery system. Without internal follow-up, service recovery is a one-shot, spray-and-pray activity—not part of a planned system of problem solving and problem elimination.

SERVICE RECOVERY ASSUMPTIONS

Whether you choose to use our six-step process or create your own recovery process (we've seen others equally serviceable), there are seven assumptions or axioms that seem common to service recovery processes that work well:

- The problem can and will be fixed.
- Fix the person, then the problem.
- Customers have clear recovery expectations.
- Customers expect you to care.
- Recovery is psychological as well as physical.
- Work in a spirit of partnership.
- Create a planned process.

The Problem Can and Will Be Fixed

Customers come to you clearly expecting that you will fix the problems they report. The data are clear: Dodge this responsibility or slide through a loophole, and the customer is history. As Professor Berry and his associates put it: "The customer expects you to do it right the first time. If you don't, you had better do it very, very right the second time around. There *are* no third opportunities."

Great customer handling skills complement, but never substitute for, fixing the customer's problem. Customers are very sensitive to being "techniqued" rather than actually helped.

Fix the Person, Then the Problem

The service representative who answers the upset, screaming customer with a bored, "Your account number, please" hasn't learned that recovery has an inherent order dictated by "psycho-logic" not "systems logic." We found in a variety of situations that dealing with the customer *first* and the technical problem second resulted in more satisfaction for the repair customer and a shorter repair call. In one study we found that letting the customer control the order of discussion during the problem reporting process, rather than forcing the caller through a standardized algorithm, "Zip code, area code, last name first, middle initial, first name last, please" brought the average call time *down* by 10 percent.

The customer who has been living with the problem wants an opportunity to tell his or her story directly to the service rep, regardless of how much the service representative already knows about the problem. This is not the time for the service representative to lecture the customer about proper procedure. The time to tell the customer what to do next time is after the problem is fixed and sensitivities are lowered.

Customers Have Clear Recovery Expectations

Just as customers have expectations of service in general, they have specific recovery expectations that must be researched and understood. As we suggested earlier, these expectations cover process, style of communication, and atonement. These expectations fall into five categories or five factors that, according to the Berry, Zeithaml, and Parasuraman research,[15] cover 80 percent of the differences between high and low customer satisfaction scores. These factors are:

- **Reliability:** The ability to provide what was promised, dependably and accurately.

- **Assurance:** Knowledge and courtesy of employees, and their ability to convey trust and confidence.

- **Tangibles:** The physical facilities and equipment, and appearance of personnel.

- **Empathy:** The degree of caring and individual attention provided to customers.

- **Responsiveness:** The willingness to help customers and provide prompt service.

Customers Expect You to Care

Customers expect *someone* from your organization to be as concerned over their problems they are. Customers are experts at detecting an "Oh damn, another complaining customer!" attitude. Generally, this means they expect to hear concern in the service people's voices, experience a sense of haste in your organization's problem-solving attempts, and to be given an explanation of how the problem occurred—*after* a fix is set in motion.

Recovery Is Psychological as Well as Physical

Customers who have a problem with your product or service, as we have said, expect you to solve the problem. Just as important, but less easy, for customers to articulate, is the need to be "fixed" psychologically. Often a customer who has a bad experience with your company or product loses faith in your reliability—your ability to deliver what you promised. The repair person who goes straight to the copier or laser printer, completes the repair task, and quietly leaves for the next call may be practicing good technical work-unit-per-hour management, but not good recovery. The customer contact person who needed to use the broken machine and was under pressure to get it fixed needs to be "repaired" as well. If nothing more, the service person needs to give the contact person an opportunity to vent his or her pent-up frustration. It's part of the job.

Work in a Spirit of Partnership

Our research suggests strongly that customers who *participate* in the problem-solving effort are more satisfied with the problem resolution. There *are*, however, limits and provisos to this dictum. When the company clearly causes the problem, asking the customer what he or she would like to see happen next gives the customer a sense of regaining control. That regained sense of control can be vital to calming customers who feel that the organization treated them unjustly or in some way abused them.

When the customer clearly caused the problem, asking him or her to do something to help facilitate solving the problem is appropriate and increases the probability that the customer will feel satisfied with the solution. The solution, in both situations, becomes *our* solution, not *your* solution.

Critical to creating a sense of partnership is the way you invite the customer into the problem-solving process. The query "what do you want me to do about it?" may be seen as shifting the responsibility for managing the service recovery process back onto the customer.

Create a Planned Process

Airlines and hotels overbook. Trains and planes have weather delays and cancellations. If uncontrollable conditions can cause problems for your customers, creating a planned process makes imminent sense. However you must institute and apply the planned process in a highly responsive, customer-sensitive fashion. Customers remember uncaring, robotic recovery long after they forget the incident that necessitated the solution.

It is important that frontline service employees know what you expect planned recovery to look like and where the limits to recovery lie. It is also critically important that they regularly practice implementing the plan. Customers remember two things from well-designed and well-implemented planned recovery: the quality of the solutions offered and the skill of the people offering it. Of the two, the latter is the *most* memorable.

Remember: When the customer is most upset and unsure, you want *your* people to be their most calm, confident, and competent. That's the purpose of planned and practiced recovery.

4

MANAGING THE
SERVICE RECOVERY EFFORT

In a small organization with a handful of sales or service people, the six-step process described in Chapter 3, plus a little coaching and supervision, should be adequate for improving customer satisfaction with problem solving. Improving service recovery in a larger company with many locations is a more daunting process. Creating distinctive service recovery in a large organization requires management to create a social or cultural milieu that supports and promotes service recovery or customer problem solving as an important activity. They must also create vehicles that communicate the core of the service recovery guidelines and reinforce the service recovery message.

CREATING THE CULTURE

Through our consulting work and via an organizational survey called the Service Management Practices Inventory (SMPI®)* with a 70,000 respondent database, we have looked carefully at the issues that inhibit and the factors that promote distinctive service recovery. We have found that customers give the highest recovery

*See the appendix for a self-assessment adapted in part from the SMPI.

scores to organizations where the following five things seem to be in place internally:

- Focused recovery training.
- Recovery standards.
- The organization is "easy to complain to."
- Frontline employees are part of a system.
- Employees believe they are part of a quality-conscious organization.

Focused Recovery Training

The company trains employees in the five points of handling customer problems and continually apprises them of the most common problems customers encounter. Also, employees must already have or continuously develop skills to enlist the customer in generating acceptable solutions to the problem or complaint.

Interestingly, some organizations believe that discussing service recovery sends the message that errors are OK and that this detracts from a total quality, zero defects effort. In practice we've found just the opposite, however. A focused recovery system shows employees proof that the organization is serious about service quality; so serious that it is making a significant effort to solve problems and cater to upset customers.

Recovery Standards

Formal standards and informal norms reinforce the message that solving customer problems quickly, with a minimum of inconvenience for the customer, is important. Also part of this system is a norm, implied or explicitly stated, that frontline people are encouraged to go above and beyond for the customer. Often the company communicates this message by recognizing employees who have saved an upset customer relationship or who simply have gone above and beyond for a customer and been cited for it by the customer. At Federal Express Corporation employees who are commended by customers through letter or phone call receive "Bravo Zulu" awards (letters of commendation) in front of their peers. Also, the company records the performance in their personnel record. Other organizations, such as the B.T. Miller Corporation of Arlington, Texas, one of the country's most profitable and successful office supply companies, regularly use bulletin boards and the company newsletter to communicate about employee heroics and their outcomes.

Some organizations also attach financial rewards to above-and-beyond performance. We see no evidence in our data that such remuneration is important. We have come to believe that recognition serves as an effective reward and reinforcement of the group norm and is a sufficient motivator.

The Organization Is "Easy to Complain To"

We find that in recovery-oriented organizations there are systems policies and procedures in place that make it easy for customers to report problems or complaints and for employees to respond. The TARP organization has found that the primary reason customers do not complain to an organization is that they don't know how. They have no idea how to effectively lodge a complaint or report a problem. In addition, TARP found that as many as half of all customer complaints are lodged with employees who cannot effectively respond to the complaint.

We have known for some time that policies and procedures that narrowly define employee responsibilities and roles severely limit the initiative and risk an employee will take for a complaining customer. More recently, we are finding that technological limits, in the form of poor telephone, E-mail, customer communication systems, and limited computer information systems severely limit service-employee problem solving. Organizations such as Lands' End, L.L. Bean, USAA, and others owe much of their success in solving customer problems to facilitated, state-of-the-art communication and information technology.

Frontline Employees Are Part of a System

The key to recovery is handling the problem on first contact. This requires that frontline employees have the tools, empowerment, and training to handle almost every issue.

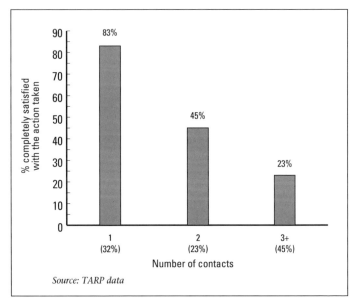

Source: TARP data

Figure 3. Impact of Number of Contacts Made on Satisfaction with Action Taken

Figures 3 and 4, from a TARP insurance company study, illustrate the damage that takes place when the customer must have more than one contact or talk to more than one person.

Also, TARP has found that handling on first contact is at least 90% cheaper than having the customer go to a second employee or having to call the customer back.

In organizations that have successful recovery systems, frontline employees are confident that problems they solve will stay solved and that others in the organization will work as hard as they on the customer's problem. Frontline employees believe that the company supports their recovery efforts. If they need to refer the customer to another unit, that unit will address the problem with the same skill, dispatch, and professionalism

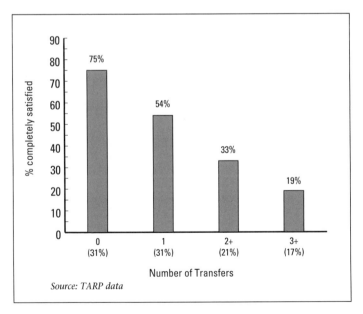

Source: TARP data

Figure 4. Impact of Number of Transfers Made on Satisfaction with Action Taken

that the company expects of them. In our surveys, positive responses to the statement "I know that the customer will receive great service if I have to refer him/her to another department for help," tend to correlate very highly to overall positive customer perceptions of an organization's recovery efforts.

Support can take many forms, from supervisory encouragement and backing to recognition for recovery well done. One effective form of support allows frontline employees to meet regularly, without a manager present, to discuss difficult customer problems and to share their successes and failures in dealing with these problems. Organizations like the account services group of American Express credit such meetings with motivating employees and keeping them on the cutting edge of customer problem solving. Employees often see this as a sign that they are indeed empowered to do whatever needs to be done to solve customer problems—and to be creative in their delivery of solutions.

Employees Believe They Are Part of a Quality-Conscious Organization

In good service recovery companies frontline employees are confident that everyone is as concerned about quality and customer satisfaction as they are. They believe that there is consensus in the organization around the importance of customer retention and the value of recovery efforts to the organization's retention efforts. In organizations where sales and customer service tend to operate independently, it is important that frontline service people believe that the sales force is as concerned with problem solving as they are. We noticed in several instances that informal communications between individual sales people and frontline service people promote this sense of mutual concern with recovery and retention. We also found in several studies that customers are very impressed when sales people know about the problems they encountered and the state of the resolution. This is particularly pronounced for organizations where sales and services are ostensibly separate functions. We found that five factors tend to inhibit or, in some cases limit, organizational efforts to support service recovery and use it as a marketplace distinguisher. As a group, they are distinguished by their impact on the frontline service providers. The five factors are:

- unclear focus
- restrictive rules
- low level of skill
- trying and failing
- no payoff

UNCLEAR FOCUS

Employees need a clear vision of what the organization is attempting to accomplish *for customers* and how it wants customers to perceive that mission. If recovery is to distinguish the company or be an important retention tactic, employees need to know:

- why recovery is important
- what role the employees play in creating recovery
- what a job well done looks like through the customer's eyes

Horst Schultze, CEO of Baldrige Award-winning Ritz-Carlton Hotels, calls it "Enlisting your employees in your vision."

RESTRICTIVE RULES

A colleague contends that if you put the best-trained, most highly motivated employees in a system that punishes initiative or rule-bending for customers, they will look like the system in 90 days. It is important that the formal rules and policies and procedures *reflect* the processes, allowable ways, and flexibility necessary for a recovery effort.

LOW LEVEL OF SKILL

A study done by *Training Magazine* found that the average frontline service employee receives about $2.80 worth of training in the average year. Compare that to the 40 hours of training the average Ritz Carlton or Federal Express employee receives and the contrast is obvious. Employees charged with service recovery need a capacity to respond to customers beyond set rules and regulations. Employees in a service recovery environment need to know the organization's products and services intimately as well as the ins and outs of who does what for whom within the organization. They need to be among the most knowledgeable and clever in the organization.

TRYING AND FAILING

Empowerment begins with error. How a company treats service providers when they make mistakes in the customer's favor sets the tone for how far an employee will go to solve a customer's problem. Protection from punishment encourages risk-taking. This is *not* to suggest that service recovery comes from giving frontline employees unlimited license. But it *does* suggest that they need responsible freedom to make judgments, and support when their judgments are occasionally wrong.

NO PAYOFF

As we already mentioned, recognition on a wide scale cements the recovery effort. Praise without critique, and group celebration for improvements in retention statistics, energize and sustain a recovery system.

A final factor we see repeatedly that is associated with effective recovery is the role model that supervision and management set. Organizations where employees report that their managers set the tone and lead the way through their personal behavior almost invariably receive rave reviews from customers.

5

CREATING A
SERVICE RECOVERY SYSTEM

We have alluded several times to the idea that service recovery is a system composed of multiple components, only one of which is the actual recovery transaction between the customer and a representative of your organization. For service recovery to be more than a process for cleaning up after slapdash service and products that perform poorly, it must also serve as a resource for systematic improvement of primary processes that create products and services. Berry and Parasuraman[16] have identified three major outcomes of an effective service recovery system:

1. It identifies service problems.

2. It resolves problems effectively.

3. The organization learns from the recovery experience.

These three outcomes provide a robust framework. Figure 5 shows an adaptation based on the guidance this framework provides. It details the framework as we interpret it. The goal is to suggest the activities and mechanisms an organization needs to put in place to maximize the service recovery effort.

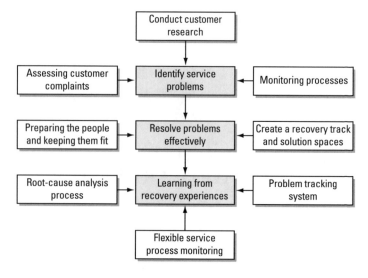

Source: Adapted from Berry and Parasuraman,
Marketing Services, *The Free Press, 1991.*

**Figure 5. Activities that Maximize the Service Recovery
Effort**

IDENTIFYING SERVICE PROBLEMS

The purposes of the process to identify problems are
to capture historic and emerging information about organizational errors and problems in need of correcting and
expunging, and to make sure that customers with problems are managed effectively. The three basic streams of
this information are customer research, assessing customer complaints, and monitoring processes.

Customer Research

This is customer (not market) research focused on customers with complaints about the organization's products

or services. The search is for complaints not commonly reported and recovery expectations not previously understood. It is a search for the causes of customer acceptance, satisfaction, or disappointment with recovery and the causes. The keys to effective customer recovery research are to look for the unfound, the unusual, and the unexpected. Asking unusual questions helps, as does looking at and analyzing historical customer complaint and disappointment information in unusual ways. Also helpful are focusing on customer satisfaction and dissatisfaction with problem resolution. For example, one managed-care firm in the Northwestern United States found that complaints to its member relations group represented only 15 percent of actual customer complaints. The other 85 percent were voiced to doctors and clinic staff members who, overwhelmingly, did nothing with the information.

Effective tools for researching customer problems are focus groups, paper and pencil, telephone surveys, customer intercepts, employee logs, and mystery shoppers.

Assessing Customer Complaints

It is important to examine incoming customer complaints in a timely fashion to spot emerging problem trends and newly developing delivery-system deficiencies. The complaint-handling system is also a vehicle for spotting and thinking through new situations that service reps need to respond to in the near future. Early warning, action planning, and planned follow-up opportunity are the keys to real-time customer complaint assessment.

Monitoring Processes

Monitoring the process of serving customers and of handling customer complaints is important for keeping the transaction quality clean, positive, and on track. The goal is to look for spots where the systems for serving customers and creating recovery are bent, if not broken. It is about finding real and potential fail points and repairing them. Good tools for the job are mystery shopping, simple observation, and the creation of detailed service blueprints and maps.

RESOLVING PROBLEMS EFFECTIVELY

Prepare People and Keep Them Fit

Good recovery depends on finding, training, and retaining good people. Good people are those with the strength to withstand the barbs of unhappy customers and with the learned cool to search for solutions to customer problems in the customer's presence.

Effective preparation of good people begins with hiring. *Hire* the right people. *Screen* technical people for customer skills. *Train* employees in the psychology of customers, problem solving, customer handling, and product knowledge. *Empower* employees to deal with customer problems and to resolve them on the spot. Give them the time and tools to do the job the way you want it done. Technology is essential. *Reward* and *recognize* excellent performance.

Create a Recovery Track and Solution Spaces

The focus of the recovery track is to help frontline service representatives heal broken customer relationships and keep customers. The process, such as our six-step process to service recovery, emphasizes: apology, listening, empathy skills, rapid resolution, added-value treatment, compensation, and, where useful, customer education.

Solution spaces provide a specific plank protocol or model to follow in specific service-breakdown situations.

For example, most airlines have a protocol for over-booked flights. The protocol tells employees exactly what types of compensation and alternative arrangements to make for bumped passengers. A good solution space matrix suggests atonement that is valuable and real. When airlines find enough volunteers to avoid bumping unwilling travelers it is because their atonement offer (free tickets or travel vouchers) is a good balance for the inconvenience of taking a different, often later, flight.

For the solution to be effective in the eyes of the customer, the deliverer must not use it as an excuse to treat the breakdown in a trivial or off-handed fashion. The apology for inconvenience, the problem correction, and the offer of compensation must be treated seriously.

LEARNING FROM RECOVERY EXPERIENCE

An effective service recovery learning loop sends information about product and service problems back into the product and service production system.

The methods described earlier feed data into tracking and root-cause analysis processes that create usable information for confirming or correcting the functioning of the product and service delivery production system.

This organizational learning component has several features:

- A problem-tracking system
- A root-cause analysis process
- Flexible service process monitoring

Interestingly, according to the TARP NASM Study—Executive Summary, only 11 percent of American companies have all three.

Problem-Tracking System

The focus of a recovery tracking system is measurement of the customer retention and delivery improvement effort. It should answer two questions:

- Does the problem-resolution process actually result in customer satisfaction and retention?

- Does feeding product and service breakdown information back to the production cycle result in improved products and service delivery?

Keys to an effective problem-tracking system are contact-tracking, assessment of problem resolution satisfaction, and problem-trend analysis.

It is also important that feedback from the recovery system to product and service production be "decriminalized." That is, information from the recovery system must be seen as valuable and valued.

A Root-Cause Analysis Process

Whether housed within the service recovery function or within the system that creates services and products, information from the recovery process should feed into a root-cause analysis process. To create acceptance of the information that goes from the recovery function to a production function, a joint-problem analysis process is preferable.

Keys to an effective root-cause analysis system are training in analytical techniques, time available for data analysis, and permission to make process improvement suggestions.

Flexible Service Process Monitoring

A good service recovery system frequently uncovers service delivery fail points that heretofore were unidentified and thus unmonitored. The service recovery function, therefore, must have the flexibility and permission to establish monitoring or feedback systems of these previously unmonitored fail points.

Keys to monitoring service processes are the skills to establish such systems within the recovery system and the permission to create new monitoring efforts as need is perceived.

6

SUMMARY

In the search for total quality management, zero-defect products and services, and high-value customer outcomes, errors do occasionally happen through no fault of the customer or provider, and they have a significant impact on customer retention. In some versions of total quality, errors seen as random are dismissed as if they are not relevant, since they are not systematic or amenable to eradication through the tools of statistical process control, wishbone diagramming, and so forth. But regardless of the source of an error, a customer is involved and a customer is at risk. Service recovery is a process designed to save the at-risk customer and, secondarily, to feed useful information for problem prevention back into an organization's quality management and quality assurance processes.

In summary our key points are:

1. Recovery, or returning an aggrieved customer to a state of satisfaction after a service or product breakdown, has a critical economic impact on your business.

2. Breakdown involves customer expectations of both outcomes and processes.

3. Recovering well when things have gone wrong

increases customer loyalty and decreases marketing expenses.

4. Only your customer can tell you how annoying or victimizing a particular service breakdown has been. Only your customer can determine when appropriate recovery has occurred.

5. Planned service recovery ensures that each breakdown is handled creatively and satisfies customer and organizational needs.

6. You can—and should—plan for the unexpected.

7. When problems occur, customers expect you to apologize, give them a fair fix, treat them like you care, and atone for injuries.

8. "Fix the person, then the problem" is a good rule unless you can't fix the problem. Planned recovery helps you do both—and do them well.

9. It is critical to identify recurring problems so that you can make changes and corrections in production and service delivery systems.

10. Planned service recovery improves overall service quality awareness and motivates employees to work on the customer's behalf to solve problems.

Creating service quality is a journey, not a destination. In our competitive world, customer expectations constantly change and rise—due, in part, to the never-ending contest to be first in the customer's esteem and first in the marketplace. Service recovery, done well, energizes the effort to create quality service and motivates service employees to "keep on keeping on" on the customer's behalf. Done right, service recovery tells the customer "We're here to set things right when they go wrong. No problem." William James, the father of modern American psychology, commented that "The deepest principle of human nature is a craving to be appreciated." That's true of our customers, true of our peers, and true of our associates. And nothing is more appreciated than a problem solved faster, easier, and more effectively than a customer dared hope.

APPENDIX:
HOW READY ARE YOU TO
RECOVER WHEN THINGS GO
WRONG FOR CUSTOMERS?

These self-assessment questions are adapted from the Service Management Practices Inventory, a database of over 150 questions and responses from 37,000 managers and customer service employees in more than 200 companies; and from the Recovery Readiness Inventory.

This is an opportunity for you to be as brutally frank and honest as you can stand being about your department's—or group's—shortcomings. At the same time, it is important to take credit for the good and right things you are already doing.

When you have completed the assessment, review your responses using the "Scoring Master" answer sheet (see p. 56). Then decide on appropriate improvement actions.

SYSTEMS, POLICIES AND PROCEDURES

The extent to which our systems, policies and procedures make it easy for frontline and support employees

Service Management Practices Inventory (SMPI) and Recovery Readiness Inventory (RRI) are trademarks of Performance Research Associates Inc. and Questar Data Systems Inc.

to deliver quality service in the face of a service breakdown, and the degree to which systems, policies, and procedures are seen to support rather than inhibit good service recovery.

1. Assisting customers with problems is a clear priority in our company.

   YES ___   NO ___

2. The way my department/unit/division is organized makes it easy for employees to solve customer problems quickly.

   YES ___   NO ___

3. The way we are organized makes it easy for customers to reach the right individual or area when they have a problem or question.

   YES ___   NO ___

4. We provide a "service guarantee" to customers; it is well known among our customers.

   YES ___   NO ___

5. My department/unit/division has clearly defined procedures for what to do when mistakes are made or errors are discovered.

   YES ___   NO ___

6. Customers experiencing problems can start the recovery process with a single contact; our "system" doesn't require the customer to make multiple contacts to report a problem or get action.

   YES ___   NO ___

7. When problem solving takes longer than the initial contact, we have a system in place for staying in touch with the customer and updating him or her on the progress of the recovery process.

    YES __   NO __

8. Frontline employees are allowed to make value-added "atonement" gestures—such as comp'ing a repair or extending a subscription—at their own discretion.

    YES __   NO __

9. All frontline and support employees know what they personally can do to solve customer problems.

    YES __   NO __

10. When a customer problem is corrected, I am confident that it will not reoccur...at least not for *this* customer.

    YES __   NO __

11. We have a formal process for collecting data on errors, complaints and comments, analyzing their significance, and modifying our systems accordingly.

    YES __   NO __

12. Our hiring criteria for frontline service people emphasizes "working with customer" skills, as well as technical skills and knowledge.

    YES __   NO __

Summary

My score on Systems, Policies, and Procedures: _____
Improvements I need to make:

EVALUATING SERVICE PERFORMANCE

The degree to which we establish clear, customer-focused standards for service recovery, and the extent to which we measure quality of work performance against those standards.

1. My department/unit/division has set clear standards for response time to customer complaints, questions, inquiries and other contacts and correspondence.

   YES __ NO __

2. Our standards are based on customer input rather than on internally generated technical criteria.

   YES __ NO __

3. We post our performance-to-standards data on a regular basis.

   YES __ NO __

4. For us, regular means:

   DAILY __ WEEKLY __ MONTHLY __

   QUARTERLY __ NOT AT ALL __

5. Everyone who works for me meets or exceeds those standards on a regular basis.

   YES __ NO __

6. Our standards reflect "customer fixing" activities and outcomes as well as "problem fixing" activities and outcomes.

   YES __ NO __

7. We ask customers to evaluate us on the results of every service recovery effort.

YES __ NO __

8. Customer evaluations include some elements of each of the following: reliability, responsiveness, assurance, tangibles, and empathy.

YES __ NO __

9. We "shop" and/or do "ride alongs" with service representatives on a regular basis (at least twice a year).

YES __ NO __

10. Some of our standards are tailored to specific customers with unique requirements.

YES __ NO __

Summary

My score on Evaluating Service Performance: _____

Improvements I need to make:

CUSTOMER FOCUS AND COMMITMENT

The degree to which we as an organization, and our employees as individuals, think about, focus on, and are concerned with satisfying our customers on a day to day basis.

1. Employees feel empowered to take action to fulfill out of the ordinary customer needs or solve unusual problems without special permission.

    YES ___   NO ___

2. Employees feel a personal sense of pride and ownership when they are able to use their service recovery skills to help customers.

    YES ___   NO ___

3. Employees are not "afraid" to ask customers about their satisfaction with our products and services; employees are comfortable acting on information about customer dissatisfaction.

    YES ___   NO ___

4. We make a policy of asking customers what they expect from us when problems occur.

    YES ___   NO ___

5. Our current standards are a result of asking customers what they expect of us when problem situations occur.

    YES ___   NO ___

6. There is good teamwork between individual employees and departments when solving customer problems.

   YES __   NO __

7. We almost always follow up with customers to be sure fixed problems stay fixed.

   YES __   NO __

8. It is not at all unusual for employees to spot and solve potential customer problems before the customer is even aware of them.

   YES __   NO __

9. Everyone in my organization understands that retaining current customers through effective problem solving is every bit as important as gaining new customers.

   YES __   NO __

10. Everyone in my part of the organization knows the "dollars and sense" of customer retention.

   YES __   NO __

Summary

My score on Customer focus and Commitment: _____
Improvements I need to make:

RECOGNIZING AND REWARDING SERVICE

The degree to which individual and group efforts to prevent, spot and solve customer problems are recognized and rewarded in my department/unit/division.

1. Managers and supervisors in my department/unit/division constantly look for evidence of employees who take a personal interest in resolving customer complaints and problems.

   YES __   NO __

2. Such employees are frequently "spot" rewarded in a tangible way for their efforts.

   YES __   NO __

3. Employees who practice good service recovery are held up as role models for other employees.

   YES __   NO __

4. Employees who err while working on behalf of a customer are confident that they will not be "punished."

   YES __   NO __

5. Employees know that their ability to prevent, spot, and solve customer problems plays an important part in performance reviews and advancement decisions.

   YES __   NO __

6. We have a formal system that allows employees to recognize and thank other employees for their assistance in solving a customer's problem.

   YES __   NO __

7. We have a formal system that encourages our customers to recognize employees for their assistance in preventing or correcting a service breakdown.

YES __   NO __

Summary

My score on Recognizing and Rewarding Service: _____

Improvements I need to make:

TRAINING AND SUPPORTING

The degree to which employees are trained and supported to do what is necessary to meet customers' needs and solve customers' problems.

1. We encourage employees to go "above and beyond" for customers.

    YES __   NO __

2. Employees believe that their "above and beyond" efforts for customers are recognized and valued.

    YES __   NO __

3. We train customer contact people in the "How-Tos" of:

    A. Listening carefully and fully to customers.

    YES __   NO __

    B. "Reading" customer types and/or moods.

    YES __   NO __

    C. Making a positive impression during problem fixing.

    YES __   NO __

    D. Dealing with angry customers.

    YES __   NO __

4. We take specific actions to help employees deal with the stress that comes from customer contact.

   YES __   NO __

5. When an employee does not feel capable of dealing with a particular customer or customer problem, he or she knows exactly whom to ask for assistance.

   YES __   NO __

6. Managers and supervisors in my department/unit/ division regularly meet one-on-one with employees to coach them on service recovery skills.

   YES __   NO __

7. Employees regularly meet together—without a manager present—to discuss "tough" customer problems and to exchange information on solving customer problems.

   YES __   NO __

Summary

My score on Training and Supporting: _____

Improvements I need to make:

HOW READY ARE YOU TO RECOVER WHEN THINGS GO WRONG FOR CUSTOMERS?

Scoring Master

Systems, Policies, and Procedures		Evaluating Service Performance		Customer Focus and Commitment		Recognizing and Rewarding Service		Train and Support	
Yes	No	Yes	No	Yes	No	Yes	No	Yes	No
1. 2	0	1. 3	0	1. 3	0	1. 2	0	1. 3	0
2. 3	0	2. 2	0	2. 2	0	2. 2	0	2. 2	0
3. 3	0	3. 2	0	3. 2	0	3. 2	0	3. A=2, B=1, C=2, D=3 Max=8	
4. 2	0	4. 2 for D/M/W 1 for Q		4. 3	0	4. 2	0	4. 2	0
5. 3	0	5. 3	0	5. 2	0	5. 3	0	5. 2	0
6. 2	0	6. 2	0	6. 3	0	6. 2	0	6. 2	0
7. 2	0	7. 2 for *Every* 1 for *Majority*		7. 2	0	7. 2	0	7. 2	0
8. 2	0	8. 2 for all 5 1 for 3 of 5		8. 2	0				
9. 2	0	9. 2	0	9. 1	0				
10. 3	0	10. 3	0	10. 1	0				
11. 2	0								
12. 2	0								
28	0	21	0	21	0	15	0	21	0
Minimum Comfort Zone: 22		Minimum Comfort Zone: 16		Minimum Comfort Zone: 16		Minimum Comfort Zone: 12		Minimum Comfort Zone: 12	

Recovery Report Card

91-106	A+		80-84	B+
85-90	A		75-79	B

Less then 79 points: "Not any worse than anybody else—and not any better."

© Performance Reasearch Associates. Inc.

NOTES

1. John Goodman, "Don't Fix the Product, Fix the Customer," *Quality Review* (Fall, 1988): 8–11.

2. Ibid.

3. C.R. Bell and R. Zemke, "Service Breakdown: The Road to Recovery," *Management Review*, (October, 1987).

4. Ibid.

5. Jean M. Otte, Corporate Vice President, Quality Management, National Car Rental System, Inc., presentation to Minnesota Chapter, Society of Consumer Affairs Professionals in Business (June 8, 1992).

6. This research was initiated by an executive of the hotel corporation as part of a Service Management operations course at a local university. The corporation now uses these data to justify making the bottom 5 percent of its franchises (as determined by CSI) "available to the industry." They simply can't afford to keep properties that drive away customers.

7. *Consumer Complaint Handling in America: An Update Study, Part II,* conducted by Technical Assistance Research Programs Institute for the U.S. Office of Consumer Affairs (March 31, 1986): 50.

8. Unpublished study conducted by Performance Research Associates, Inc.

9. J. Goodman et al., "Setting Priorities for Satisfaction Improvement," in *Service Wisdom: Creating and Maintaining the Customer Service Edge,* R. Zemke and C.R. Bell, eds. (Minneapolis: Lakewood Books, 1990). First published in *The Quality Review* (Winter, 1987).

10. Frederick Reichheld and W. Earl Sasser, "Zero Defections: Quality Comes to Services," *Harvard Business Review* (Sept-Oct, 1990): 105.

11. J. Goodman, "Don't Fix the Product, Fix the Customer," *Quality Review* (Fall, 1988).

12. Linda Cooper and Associates (Evanston, Ill.), "Top Ten Service Attributes of Importance to Customers" (seminar presentation).

13. In one survey we conducted, we found that asking the customer how they would like the problem solved made a significant difference between a satisfied and a very satisfied customer attitude toward a company's problem-fixing effort.

14. Philip Newbold and Diane Serbin Stover, Memorial Hospital, South Bend, Ind., *Health Care Forum Journal* (December, 1994).

15. Leonard Berry, Valarie Zeithaml, and A. Parasuraman, "Five Imperatives for Improving Service Quality," *Sloan Management Review* (Summer, 1990):29.

16. Leonard Berry and A. Parasuraman, *Marketing Services* (New York: Free Press, 1991).

FURTHER READING

Karl Albrecht and Ron Zemke, *Service America! Doing Business In The New Economy* (Homewood: Business One Irwin, 1985).

Kristin Anderson, *Great Customer Service On The Telephone* (New York: AMACOM Books, 1992).

Kristin Anderson, and Ron Zemke, *Delivering Knock Your Socks Off Service* (New York: AMACOM Books, 1991).

Chip R. Bell, *Customers As Partners: Building Relationships That Last* (San Francisco: Berrett Koehler, 1994).

Chip R. Bell, and Ron Zemke, *Managing Knock Your Socks Off Service* (New York: AMACOM Books, 1992).

Chip R. Bell, and Ron Zemke, "Do Service Procedures Tie Employee Hands?" *Personnel Journal* (September, 1988).

Thomas K. Connellan, and Ron Zemke, *Sustaining Knock Your Socks Off Service* (New York: AMACOM Books, 1991).

Ron Zemke, *The Service Edge: 101 Companies That Profit From Customer Care* (New York: New American Library, 1989).

Ron Zemke, and Chip R. Bell, *Service Wisdom* (Minneapolis, Minn.: Lakewood Books, 1990).

Ron Zemke, and Chip R. Bell, "Service Recovery: Doing it Right the Second Time," *Training* (June 1990).

ADDITIONAL RESOURCES

OOPS! Time For Service Recovery, hosted by Ron Zemke, and Chip R. Bell. Salenger Films/Video, Santa Monica, Calif. 1991.

Sox Off Service, four-part video series staring Lily Tomlin, Mentor Media Inc., Los Angeles, Calif. 1993.

Ron Zemke, and Chip R. Bell, *Managing Extraordinary Service*, 3-day workshop for middle managers, Kaset International, Tampa, Fla.

Services Management Practices Inventory, in-depth service quality satisfaction survey instrument for both internal and external customers, Performance Research Associates, Minneapolis, Minn.

Customers From Hell and The Ten Deadly Sins of Customer Care, a new board game designed to train front line service people in the how to's of dealing with difficult customers, Performance Research Associates, Minneapolis, Minn.

Creating and Managing Distinctive Quality Service, live, 60-minute video concert focusing on service quality and the six key components of building service partnership, Performance Research Associates, Minneapolis, Minn.

ABOUT THE AUTHOR

Ron Zemke is president of Performance Research Associates, Inc., a consulting firm specializing in service quality audits, and service management programs. His clients have included Citibank, Microsoft, GTE, 3M, Ford Motor Company, General Motors—Canada, Steelcase, General Mills, Pitney Bowes Corporation, and Union Carbide.

In addition to his consulting work, Mr. Zemke is a well-known business writer. As senior editor of Minneapolis-based *Training* magazine and editor of *The Service Edge* newsletter, he has won many awards for his writing. In addition, he is the author or coauthor of 11 books. *Sustaining Knock Your Socks Off Service* was named one of the 30 best business books of 1993 by Executive Book Summaries. Other titles include *Service America! Doing Business in the New Economy; Managing Knock Your Socks Off Service; The Service Edge: 101 Companies That Profit from Customer Care,* and *Stressless Selling.*

Mr. Zemke was the recipient of the 1994 Mobius Award for his contributions to the customer service profession. He conducts public and private seminars each year for organizations throughout the world.

Ron Zemke, Performance Research Associates, 1820 Foshay Tower, 821 Marquette Avenue South, Minneapolis MN 55402, Telephone 612-338-8523

PRAISE FOR THE MANAGEMENT MASTER SERIES

"A rare information resource.... Each book is a gem; each set of six books a basic library.... Handy guides for success in the '90s and the new millennium."

Otis Wolkins
Vice President Quality Services/Marketing
Administration, GTE

"Productivity Press has provided a real service in its *Management Master Series*. These little books fill the huge gap between the 'bites' of oversimplified information found in most business magazines and the full-length books that no one has enough time to read. They have chosen very important topics in quality and found well-known authors who are willing to hold themselves within the 'one plane trip's worth' length limitation. Every serious manager should have a few of these in their reading backlog to help keep up with today's new management challenges."

C. Jackson Grayson, Jr.
Chairman, American Productivity & Quality Center

"The *Management Master Series* takes the Cliffs Notes approach to management ideas, with each monograph a tight 50 pages of remarkably meaty concepts that are defined, dissected, and contextualized for easy digestion."

Industry Week

"A concise overview of the critical success factors for today's leaders."

Quality Digest

"A wonderful collection of practical advice for managers."

Edgar R. Fiedler
Vice President and Economic Counsellor,
The Conference Board

"A great resource tool for business, government, and education."

Dr. Dennis J. Murray
President, Marist College

PRODUCTIVITY PRESS, Dept. BK, PO Box 13390, Portland, OR 97213-0390
Telephone: 1-800-394-6868   Fax: 1-800-394-6286

THE MANAGEMENT MASTER SERIES

The Management Master Series offers business managers leading-edge information on the best contemporary management practices. Written by respected authorities, each short "briefcase book" addresses a specific topic in a concise, to-the-point presentation, using both text and illustrations. These are ideal books for busy managers who want to get the whole message quickly.

Set 1. Great Management Ideas

Management Alert: Don't Reform—Transform!
Michael J. Kami
Transform your corporation: adapt faster, be more productive, perform better.

Vision, Mission, Total Quality: Leadership Tools for Turbulent Times
William F. Christopher
Build your vision and mission to achieve world class goals.

The Power of Strategic Partnering
Eberhard E. Scheuing
Take advantage of the strengths in your customer-supplier chain.

New Performance Measures
Brian H. Maskell
Measure service, quality, and flexibility with methods that address your customers' needs.

Motivating Superior Performance
Saul W. Gellerman
Use these key factors—non-monetary as well as monetary—to improve employee performance.

Doing and Rewarding: Inside a High-Performance Organization
Carl G. Thor
Design systems to reward superior performance and encourage productivity.

PRODUCTIVITY PRESS, Dept. BK, PO Box 13390, Portland, OR 97213-0390
Telephone: 1-800-394-6868   Fax: 1-800-394-6286

Set 2. Total Quality

The 16-Point Strategy for Productivity and Total Quality
William F. Christopher/Carl G. Thor
Essential points you need to know to improve the performance of your organization.

The TQM Paradigm: Key Ideas That Make It Work
Derm Barrett
Get a firm grasp of the world-changing ideas beyond the Total Quality movement.

Process Management: A Systems Approach to Total Quality
Eugene H. Melan
Learn how a business process orientation will clarify and streamline your organization's capabilities.

Practical Benchmarking for Mutual Improvement
Carl G. Thor
Discover a down to-earth approach to benchmarking and building useful partnerships for quality.

Mistake-Proofing: Designing Errors Out
Richard B. Chase and Douglas M. Stewart
Learn how to eliminate errors and defects at the source with inexpensive *poka-yoke* devices and staff creativity.

Communicating, Training, and Developing for
Quality Performance
Saul W. Gellerman
Gain quick expertise in communication and employee development basics.

Set 3. Customer Focus

Designing Products and Services That Customers Want
Robert King
Here are guidelines for designing customer-exciting products and services to meet the demands for continuous improvement and constant innovation to satisfy customers.

Creating Customers for Life
Eberhard E. Scheuing
Learn how to use quality function deployment to meet the demands for continuous improvement and constant innovation to satisfy customers.

Building Bridges to Customers
Gerald A. Michaelson
From the priceless value of a single customer to balancing priorities, Michaelson delivers a powerful guide for instituting a customer-based culture within any organization.

Delivering Customer Value: It's Everyone's Job
Karl Albrecht
This volume is dedicated to empowering people to deliver customer value and aligning a company's service systems.

Shared Expectations: Sustaining Customer Relationships
Wayne A. Little
How to create a process for sharing expectations and building lasting and profitable relationships with customers and suppliers that incorporates performance goals and measures.

Service Recovery: Fixing Broken Customers
Ron Zemke
Here are the guidelines for developing a customer-retaining service recovery system that can be a strategic asset in a company's total quality effort.

PRODUCTIVITY PRESS, Dept. BK, PO Box 13390, Portland, OR 97213-0390
Telephone: 1-800-394-6868   Fax: 1-800 304 6286

Set 4. Leadership (available November, 1995)

Leading the Way to Organization Renewal

Burt Nanus

How to build and steer a continually renewing and transforming organization by applying a vision to action strategy.

Checklist for Leaders

Gabriel Hevesi

Learn to focus day-to-day decisions and actions, leadership, communications, team building, planning, and efficiency.

Creating Leaders for Tomorrow

Karl Albrecht

How to mobilize all the intelligence of the organization to create value for customers.

Total Quality: A Framework for Leadership

D. Otis Wolkins

Consider the problems and opportunities in today's world of changing technology, global competition, and rising customer expectations in terms of the leadership role.

From Management to Leadership

Lawrence M. Miller

A visionary analysis of the qualities required of leaders in today's business: vision and values, enthusiasm for customers, teamwork, and problem-solving skills at all levels.

High Performance Leadership: Creating Value in a World of Change

Leonard R. Sayles

Examine the need for leadership involvement in work systems and operations technology to meet the increasing demands for short development cycles and technologically complex products and services.

PRODUCTIVITY PRESS, Dept. BK, PO Box 13390, Portland, OR 97213-0390
Telephone: 1-800-394-6868   Fax: 1-800-394-6286

ABOUT PRODUCTIVITY PRESS

Productivity Press exists to support the continuous improvement of American business and industry.

Since 1983, Productivity has published more than 100 books on the world's best manufacturing methods and management strategies. Many Productivity Press titles are direct source materials translated for the first time into English from industrial leaders around the world.

The impact of the Productivity publishing program on Western industry has been profound. Leading companies in virtually every industry sector use Productivity Press books for education and training. These books ride the cutting edge of today's business trends and include books on total quality management (TQM), corporate management, Just-In-Time manufacturing process improvements, total employee involvement (TEI), profit management, product design and development, total productive maintenance (TPM), and system dynamics.

To get a copy of the full-color catalog, call 800-394-6868 or fax 800-394-6286.

To view sample chapters and see the complete line of books, visit the Productivity Press online catalog on the Internet at *http://www.ppress.com/*

Productivity Press titles are distributed to the trade by National Book Network, 800-462-6420

TO ORDER: Write, phone, or fax Productivity Press, Dept. BK, P.O. Box 13390, Portland, OR 97213-0390, phone 800-394-6868, fax 800-394-6286. Send check or charge to your credit card (American Express, Visa, MasterCard accepted).

U.S. ORDERS: Add $5 shipping for first book, $2 each additional for UPS surface delivery. We offer attractive quantity discounts for bulk purchases of individual titles; call for more information.

ORDER BY E-MAIL: Order 24 hours a day from anywhere in the world. Use either address:

To order: *service@ppress.com*

To view online catalog on the Internet and/or to order:
  http://www.ppress.com/

INTERNATIONAL ORDERS: Write, phone, or fax for quote and indicate shipping method desired. For international callers, telephone number is 503-235-0600 and fax number is 503-235-0909. Prepayment in U.S. dollars must accompany your order (checks must be drawn on U.S. banks). When quote is returned with payment, your order will be shipped promptly by the method requested.

NOTE: Prices are in U.S. dollars and are subject to change without notice.

PRODUCTIVITY PRESS, Dept. BK, PO Box 13390, Portland, OR 97213-0390
Telephone: 1-800-394-6868   Fax: 1-800-394-6286